I have always loved the concept captured by Henry Ward Beecher, "The first hour is the rudder of the day." As an adult, I still marvel at the "new beginning" each day offers. In *The Early to Rise Experience*, Andy Traub offers a fresh approach for recapturing those special treats offered only in the first hour of the day. With a little discipline and the pattern of a new habit, you too can tap into the time-honored secret for becoming "healthy, wealthy, and wise."
> — DAN MILLER, author and life coach · 48Days.com

Finally, a book that helps me understand the struggles I have with putting to action my goal of rising early. This book gave me a new perspective on what is at stake in my decision to either get up or sleep in. Thanks, Andy, for giving me new insights on how my life can have more of what I want by following this thirty-day challenge.
> — JEFF GOINS, author · GoinsWriter.com, @JeffGoins

A few years ago, I decided to get up early in the morning to work out before my family got up, and I accidentally became a morning person. My life has been so much better since then. I wish I'd had Andy's book to help me. *The Early to Rise Experience* will take you on a thirty-day journey to becoming an early riser. Don't just read it; read it and take Andy's thirty-day challenge. You'll be so glad you did.
> — JON DALE · JonDale.com, @JonDale

Great leaders rise early, and Andy's book is a must-read for anyone who is serious about leading others. The book will change the way you lead others, because it helps you understand the first person you need to lead is yourself.

— Chris LoCurto, former vice president at Dave Ramsey, author, and leadership expert · ChrisLoCurto.com, @ChrisLoCurto

Productive days are no accident. The most successful and influential people are the ones who learn this and know the morning is where you set the tone and direct the course for your day. This book not only reveals the "why" behind rising early but also the simple steps to becoming a successful early riser and achieving your goals.

— Erik Fisher, producer of *Beyond the To-Do List* podcast @ErikjFisher

Andy's book isn't just a challenge to get yourself out of bed early every day — that would be mean. Rather, it's about changing your life to become a better person. It's a day-by-day instruction manual for a positive attitude and what you can do (and not do) to start your day off right. Andy's book challenges you to not take the easy road in life. He holds your hand and encourages you to do something positive with your life while positively affecting others in the process. Be extraordinary. Change your life. This book will help you get there.

— Daniel Gold, author, co-producer of *The Productive Life* podcast, and productivity expert · DegConsulting.net, @DEGconsulting

To my wife, Sara, and my kids: Samuel, Caroline, and Lucy.
You are the reasons I wake up every day.

HE NEEDED MORE Time

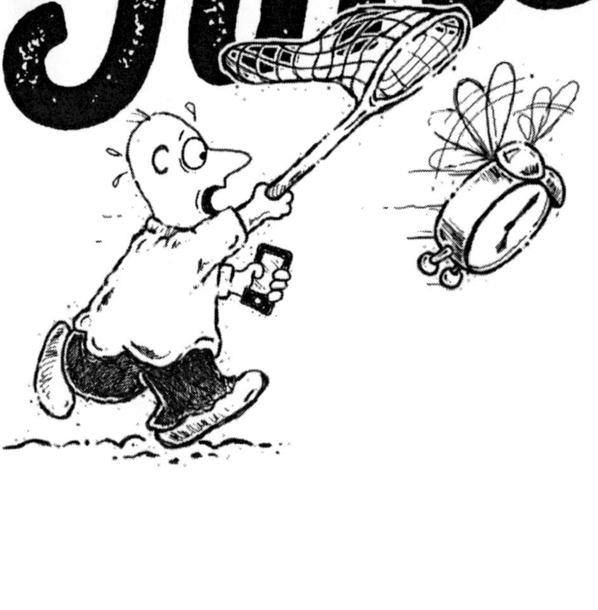

MORNING

I ran into a friend and saw he was in a rush.
I told him of a place pure, pregnant with wisdom and time.
He scoffed and waved his hand to dismiss.
He said that place had no power.
He claimed to be a person of the later hours.
He admitted he had never been to where I invited him.
He had never felt the peace of its solitude and stillness.
He rushed away, late as usual.
He needed more time.
Exactly what I had offered.
Exactly what is available to him every day.
Exactly what he had dismissed the moment before.
                                        — ANDY TRAUB, January 24, 2013

CONTENTS

INTRODUCTION

This book is about you. It's a practical guide full of tips and encouragement that will equip you to build the habit of rising early. It's a well-known fact most successful people rise early in the day, but this book isn't about them. Dead presidents aren't inspirational enough to me. I need practical advice to succeed, so that's what I am giving you. The goal of this book isn't just to help you build a habit though. **The goal is to help you change your life.**

I want you to stop being average. Average people do average stuff. As children, we don't expect to grow up to be average, but somewhere in our development, most of us become average. Average people become that way because they change their expectations. They expect to be average, and sadly, they're okay with being average. Average is pretty safe, and it's certainly very popular. In America, average is also very comfortable. Did I just describe your life? Safe, common, and comfortable? Is that what you want for your life, your marriage, your parenting, your church, and your work?

You are who you are because that's what you think you'll be. What we expect, we get — or worse. It's rare to get something better than we expect. We'll never hear a couple with a great marriage say, "We're totally shocked we're still married and in love." They don't have a great marriage because they got lucky. They are above average because they pursued above average. They pursued greatness.

Will you join me in search of a life of influence and greatness? Sometimes we will succeed and sometimes we will fail, but we will pursue more than average.

In thirty days, I believe you will be an early riser. In thirty days, you will have built a habit and, more importantly, a mindset equipping you to rise earlier than you ever imagined.

It will not be easy.

People will tell you you're crazy.

You'll want to give up.

It will likely be a lonely journey.

Sounds exciting, doesn't it? Exciting isn't the goal though; fixing your life is the goal. Fixing your life might be a bold claim, but I am not going to do it — you are. No one else can fix you. Only you can fix you, but when are you going to do it? I'll tell you when, so keep reading.

The result of rising early is being intentional about how you live.

You are pursuing greatness, because the result of rising early is being intentional about how you live. This book is very simple. It is about one thing: getting up early. Don't over-complicate the pursuit. The goal is simple, but the results will be dynamic. Your life will change, and the lives of those around you will change. The world will change because you are going to make a larger impact in your circle of influence.

You will fix many areas of your life because you're going to take control of each day. You're going to tell your day what to do, and you'll be surprised how often it obeys. You are going to become master of the life you've been given, which makes sense because it's yours.

I am a Christian, and some Christians believe Jesus should be master of their lives. This is not about dethroning the King of the Universe though; it's a practical point. Jesus doesn't brush our teeth. Jesus doesn't tap us on the shoulder and tell us it's time to get out of bed. He doesn't drive us to work. He doesn't hug our kids for us. The lives He gave us are our jobs. We're responsible for ourselves.

Your life has been given to you. You're in charge of you, and yesterday was the last day you pursued average. Today is your first day of pursuing greatness, and I believe you will achieve greatness.

The first step is simple: rise early. Let's learn how.

> — ANDY TRAUB, December 26, 2012
> Sioux Falls, South Dakota
> Current temperature: 12° F

HOW TO READ THIS BOOK

Read it in one hour or thirty-one days.
You can probably read this entire book in less than an hour, or you can take thirty-one days. Today is the first of thirty-one days, and tomorrow morning you start Day One of thirty days of encouragement on rising early.

The Early To Rise Experience is a thirty-day journey in which you will learn how to become an early riser. After reading the first few sections today, you'll come to Day One. Read Day One today so you understand the format, then read it again tomorrow morning when you rise early. Each day's passage will take you less than five minutes to read and will end with an action step for the day. You can also listen to each day's passage using links in the book or in the emails to which you may subscribe.

How early is early?
Five o'clock is my target rise time. I hit it about eighty percent of the time. Some days, I wake up at five thirty, and other days I wake up at seven thirty. I suggest starting the challenge by waking up a minimum of one hour earlier than you usually do. The purpose of this experience is to build a habit that will create change in many different areas of your life. Give yourself thirty days to build the habit. Don't try to wake up two or three hours earlier tomorrow. Don't set yourself up for failure.

Can I ease into the early morning routine?

Yes and no. You do have to start changing your bedtime routine immediately. You don't have to get up at your target rise time right away though. Set your alarm for tomorrow morning one hour earlier than you usually do. The next day, set it fifteen or thirty minutes earlier. Keep setting your alarm earlier until you find the right time for your schedule. The key to success is going to bed at the right time. This means you need to go to bed earlier starting tonight.

How will I know it's working?

If you're normal, then you likely have an unhealthy relationship with sleep. We neglect getting enough, or we binge and get too much. You will know the challenge is working when you're able to get up early, have a restful and productive morning, start your normal workday with energy, and then go to bed at a reasonable hour. If you can do this for three or four days, you will know you're in a good rhythm. If your bed time changes every night, you can't wake up on-time, or you have very little energy throughout the day, then you need to adjust your routine. The most common solution is quite simple: go to bed earlier.

The key to success

The number one reason people fail to rise early is they fail to go to bed early. Just as the key to avoiding a collision is applying the brakes early enough, we need to hit the brakes on our days (go to bed early) so we can avoid running into the lazy habit of getting up when everyone else does.

You need to go to bed earlier than usual tonight and every night going forward. If you go to bed at the regular time and expect to get up earlier, you'll probably fail every day.

If you absolutely can't get to bed early enough, don't even try to get up early. You'll probably fail to get up early, and if you do, you'll be tired all day. Get enough sleep. Go to bed early.

What do I need to do before I start?
Go to the Extras page at the end of the book and sign up for the Early to Rise emails. You can read them in your inbox, or you can listen to each day's passage. After you read or listen, close your email! It's not time to check email; it's time to work on you. Instructions for signing up are at the end of the book.

You should also take time today to:
» Pick a book or books you want to start reading.
» Pick a spot in your home that's comfortable for reading, writing, and drinking some coffee.
» Find something to write with and on: pen and paper or your laptop.
» Tell whomever you share your bed with you're going to be changing your schedule. Don't pressure him or her to join you (yet).
» Find an alarm clock or an alarm app, and make sure you understand the alarm settings. Here are links to alarm apps I like for iPhones:
  › Rise Alarm — very easy to set an alarm, and it's beautiful! EarlyToRiseBook.com/RiseAlarm
  › Sleep Cycle Alarm Clock — tracks your sleep patterns and wakes you during shallow sleep. EarlyToRiseBook.com/SleepCycle

SET YOUR **Coffee** to BREW SO IT'S READY FOR *You!*

Is there a routine I should follow?

Yes, the one that works for you! Here's one similar to mine that you may adjust accordingly:

- » Every night, prepare your morning space and set your coffee to brew so it's ready for you.
- » End your night by reading or listening to something encouraging, not by watching television (especially the news).
- » When you wake up, read that day's passage of Early to Rise, or if you've subscribed to the free daily update, check your email and read/listen to that day's passage.
- » Read, write, and listen in any combination. I turn on my computer so it starts while I get my coffee, I write for thirty to forty-five minutes, then I read and listen to books, sermons, and the like for the remainder of the time.

(More details on this are in the chapter titled "What To Do When You Get Up Early.")

You can certainly add other activities to this routine such as prayer, exercise, or pondering. Yes, pondering is an activity. More on routines in a few pages.

Where can I go to get help and encouragement?

It's a good idea to find other people to join you on this journey. You can search Twitter for mentions of #EarlyToRiseBook or you can invite some friends to join you. There is great power in creating habits and breaking habits when you are surrounded by sojourners.

In his bestselling book *The Power of Habit*, Charles Duhigg quotes Lee Ann Kaskutas, a senior scientist at the Alcohol Research Group. She explained the power groups have on helping us build habits: "There's something really powerful about groups and shared experiences. People might be skeptical about their ability to change if they're by themselves, but a group will convince them to suspend disbelief. A community creates belief."

You shouldn't try to do this alone.

Where can I get some more tips and encouragement?

For updates on the book and to read success stories from other early risers, go to EarlyToRiseBook.com. Follow Early To Rise on Twitter at Twitter.com/EarlyToRiseBook. If you need to reach me, go to EarlyToRiseBook.com/contact.

This is a thirty-day process. You are not alone, and you are going to have some success and some failure. If it was easy, you would already be doing this. It's a challenge, but you are up for it. I'm excited to be on this journey with you.

BONUS CONTENT

By purchasing this book, you are entitled to receive the full audio edition, as well as thirty days of email encouragement to help you succeed in building your Early to Rise habit.

Early To Rise extras
You're going to need more than a book to become an early riser. Habits need cues to work. A cue is a reminder to initiate an action.

I'm going to encourage you to use a few tools as cues, and I'm also going to offer you a cue. You need more than a book to build your habit because a book won't cue you. The good news is you're getting more than just a book. Anyone who purchased this book can go through The Early To Rise Experience in one or more of the following ways:

» Reading the book
» Getting an email every day for the next thirty days with the text and audio versions of each chapter
» Listening to the book all at once
» Listening to chapters one at a time

How to get your extras
To receive your extra content, visit EarlyToRiseBook.com/ Extras. When you enter your email, you will start getting each day's text and audio emailed to you for the next thirty days. Immediately after signing up, you will also have access

to the full audio of the book.

When will I get my extras?
You will have access to the full audio version immediately after signing up. The first of your daily emails should arrive the next morning before you wake up. If you don't see the first day's email, check your spam folder to see if it was sent there. Mark the message as "not spam" to avoid that happening to all of the extras. If it doesn't arrive the next day go to EarlyToRiseBook.com/contact and let me know.

The extras page has every conceivable text version of the book available for you to download: Kindle, Nook, and PDF. As a consumer, I am tired of having to buy books in different formats separately. When you buy this book, you get everything at once. Maybe I'll start a trend.

One important note
Accountability emails: If you sign up for the email accountability program after 8 p.m. CDT, you may need to wait an extra day to receive Day One via email. It's an issue with global time zones.

If you have any trouble getting the bonuses, please reach out at EarlyToRiseBook.com/Contact.

Feeding my kids
By purchasing this book, you helped feed my family. Thank you. If you want to tell others about the book, send them to EarlyToRiseBook.com/Amazon.

Now, let's start our adventure. It's time to fix your life by getting out of bed once a day.

EARLY TO RISE

WHY GET UP EARLY

My friend and New York Times bestselling author Andy Andrews studied the most successful people in history and found they had several consistent practices. From his reading, he identified seven principles and wrote about them in his book *The Traveler's Gift*. Those successful in business, marriage, service, leadership, and art were almost always early risers. Now it's time for you to join them. Dave Ramsey says if you want to be rich then do rich people stuff. Likewise, if you want all areas of your life to be rich, then do what people rich in those areas are doing.

It is not selfish to want a better life if others also benefit as a result. When I am mentally and spiritually healthy because of my early-to-rise habit, I am a better friend, father, husband, and business owner. Those closest to me reap the rewards of a better me. When you are healthy, you will bless those around you more than you are now. It's okay to focus on being a healthier person, because — admit it — you have some stuff you need to fix. So do I. Welcome to the club.

Why do you want to change your life?
Motivations matter. The reason you do something matters. My three-year-old daughter hitting her brother in the chest is quite different from an adult compressing another adult's chest to administer CPR. It's the same action but a different motive. Caroline, my oldest daughter, is motivated by revenge, while

an adult administering CPR is motivated to help save a life.

Everyone is motivated, even lazy people. They're motivated by their comfort; they want comfort, so they don't take action. Not doing something is a choice, and every choice is an action. It sounds like an oxymoron to talk about lazy people's motivations, but trust me, lazy people have motivations. What are your motivations?

Whenever we embark on a journey — whether it's starting a business, getting married, losing weight, starting a family, or driving to grandma's house for Christmas — we have a motivation. The key to taking action is recognizing why we want to take it (our motivation), then taking action even when we don't feel like it. You and I need to set up reminders of why we're getting up early.

If I told you that you could have a better marriage, would you believe me? If I told you that you could improve your mood every day, would you believe me? If I told you that you are a very disciplined person, would you believe me? I'm telling the truth.

You are capable of so much more than you are currently achieving.

You are capable of so much more than you are currently achieving, and the first step to getting there is to find motivations that will change your behaviors. It's hard to believe what we need is actually inside us, but I believe it is. You are able. You are capable.

Motivations are about our maturity. When I act mature, I am a better father, husband, church member, and friend. When I act immature, I am fairly worthless. Maturity brings everyone to a better place, while immaturity improves one person's life at the expense of others.

My favorite thinker, blogger, writer, and artist is Seth Godin. He is well-known for his marketing genius. In a recent interview, he talked about being generous with our time and talents and how that will result in greater income and influence. He made an important clarification though. When we are generous only for the sake of getting something in return, the equation breaks. We have to work to keep our motives as pure as possible or the exchange breaks down.

Our motivations matter because other people can tell what they are, and we know what they are. Our spouses, our children, our customers, and our co-workers all know our motivations. No one has completely pure motives, but there are plenty of good things to be done with mostly pure motives. When we give to give instead of giving to get, we receive something beautiful in return. I call it the art of reciprocity.

The turtle wins every time
Slow and steady will win the race to maturity. Gaining maturity is not something that can be rushed. Maturity is like emotional healing: it comes over time. There's no pill, treatment, book, exercise, or amount of money that can bring maturity or emotional healing better or more quickly than time can.

There are areas of my life in which I need to mature, but that is not a discouragement to me. We begin to grow in any area of life and in any relationship the moment we realize we need to. People who don't change their lives are those either unaware of their shortcomings or unmotivated to change the shortcomings they know about.

I have never been to an Alcoholics Anonymous meeting, but I believe the process of AA is a beautiful thing. An alcoholic must stand in front of everyone and take ownership of his current condition. "I am an alcoholic," he says. From that point forward, he knows who he is, and he knows who

he wants to be (an alcoholic in recovery). Change happens when we admit our weaknesses, but we can't fix problems we don't admit we have. Publicly declare an end to wasting your mornings. Be motivated to change because you no longer want to live that life.

Do you want to change your life? I thought so.

WHY YOU DON'T GET UP EARLY

You don't like your life. (Sorry that's depressing.)
You might not like your life very much. It's normal, actually.
Your job doesn't give you fulfillment, and the paychecks are
like cheap Band-Aids, covering but not taking away the pain.
You know you're capable of a lot more in most areas of your
life, but as the days draw to their close, you find yourself in
front of the television again. The news is on again, and the
five-day forecast is coming. That's the good part, so they save
it until the end of the show. Pathetic.

The most honest answer for why we don't wake up early is
we don't like our lives that much. We would rather be asleep
than thinking. There's nothing to wake up for. It's a form of
depression. If you sleep more than your cat, you're probably
depressed. If you wake up ten minutes before you're supposed to be at work, you probably hate your job. If you can't
get to things on time, you don't love those things.

I waited until I was married to have sex. On the way
home from our wedding reception, we didn't stop for a cup
of coffee. I was looking forward to something, so I took my
wife home, and, well, you know. When we are excited about
something, we make time for it. If you're excited about your
life, you'll stop sleeping through it.

Admit you're broken.
The best thing about admitting you are broken is you can

then go about the business of fixing yourself. Until you admit you're broken though, you won't change. You'll stay the same, or more than likely, you'll get worse. Maybe the first thing you should consider fixing is that you keep trying to fix yourself alone. You are responsible for yourself, but that doesn't mean you have to do everything on your own. If you want to fail at some things, the first step to is to do them alone. You want to fail at bench-pressing? Don't get someone to spot you. You want to fail as a parent? Don't talk to other parents. You want to hate your job? Don't talk to your boss about your thoughts and concerns.

Where do you get motivation?
When you're trying to do difficult things, emotions follow actions. Are you avoiding necessary conflict? Get it dealt with (action), and you'll feel better later (emotion). If you don't feel like doing something, you have to get over it. Do the hard things in life or your life will never get better and you'll never grow up. What do you do if you're not motivated to get up early? Wake up early. Take action, and then the emotions will show up.

My wife is angry.
As I write this, my wife is mad at me. She should be. I don't remember exactly what I did wrong — it's hard to keep track — but I was wrong. As I type this, she is lying next to me in bed exhausted from a long day of parenting our kids, and she is fuming at my continued ignorance. Things will be okay though. It will all work out because I'm next to her. I wanted to keep reading my Seth Godin book and eat some cereal, but I put the book down and avoided the urge for a snack. Those were distractions to keep me from doing what matters.

I'm next to her because I made a commitment to spend the rest of my life with her, and I intend to keep that commitment even when I don't feel like being around her or she doesn't feel like being around me. Emotions follow actions. If we take actions only when we feel like taking them, then we're immature.

You could be alone.
You might not know anyone who gets up early because they wanted to build that specific habit. It's not a popular New Year's resolution. Waking up early is scary, because it's just you and you. It's quiet, and maybe you don't know what to do when it gets quiet. Maybe you don't know where to start when it comes to making your life better, so you don't start. You certainly don't set aside time every single day to focus on yourself. That would be selfish, right? Maybe it's not selfish. Maybe it's the key to serving others by becoming the person you're capable of becoming.

How do you look at tomorrow morning?
I'm looking forward to tomorrow morning. It doesn't matter if it's Sunday night or Friday night. I'm looking forward to to-morrow. What's tomorrow for you? Are you looking forward to it? If you're not excited about tomorrow, you're normal and you need to change. Normal gets us just far enough to be disappointed we don't have more, but it gives us enough to keep us lazy. I think you want to change, and this book is going to help you do it. You might not have much to wake up for tomorrow, but I am going to ask you to take a step of faith. Show up tomorrow and start to work on the life that's kept you in bed too long. If you don't like your life, don't be hard on yourself — be hard on your routine.

Find some sojourners.

If you don't like your life, then find some sojourners. That's a fancy word for people who will go on a journey with you. If you're like most people, you're isolated and unmotivated. This journey is different though because there are others like you, and I'm going to help you find and encourage each other. I hope your sojourners are people in your family, at work, or at church, but it could be others at EarlyToRiseBook.com/ Facebook You are not alone anymore unless you choose to be.

I'm sorry you're not excited about your life enough to get out of bed early. I feel the same way sometimes, and here's the trick: Fake it until you don't have to fake it anymore. Tell yourself tomorrow is going to be awesome, then get tons of sleep and wake up early. You will build a better life, and then you won't be able to sleep in anymore because you'll be too busy living to be sleeping.

WHY YOU WANT TO GET UP EARLY

I asked people why they want to get up early. This is what they said:

So that I can get the necessary routines done to start my day and get to exercise class (or appointment) on time. I dislike putting myself in a position where I have to rush or have to leave the house with a feeling that I didn't do something necessary or important to me because "I didn't have time."
— Davi

It is a sense of freedom to accomplish so much early in the morning and still have the rest of the day ahead of me. A sunrise holds so much more promise than a sunset. — JD

To be more productive. I love having devotions (spiritual health), working out (physical health), cranking out a blog post, emptying my email inbox, and writing a new chapter to my book — and then looking up and realizing it's only 9:30 a.m. — Josh

I want to rise early because I think it will put me on a schedule that allows me to be just as productive, but a better husband and father. — Hugh

I find that the morning is so much better for me to be produc-

A SUNRISE HOLDS SO MUCH *More Promise* than a sunset.

tive. It's the only time I can be uninterrupted for the whole day, because even late at night I can be interrupted. — Alisha

The number one reason I want to wake up early is that I want to have a more positive and quieter start of the day. — Fokke

I feel better, as though I get more done. Number one is because that's my only or best time for a workout. — Jessica

I want to become an early riser because a lot of successful people I respect and admire say that it is important and have adjusted their own schedules to fit that. It seems to be the schedule the business world operates on, so I should try and adapt to that. — Don

The reason I want to rise early is that I want to discover my dream. I am using the time to pray and write. To me, finding my dream is the goal of this exercise. — Keith

To focus spiritually and intellectually for the day ahead, beginning with the end in mind (to borrow from Covey) so the day is as productive and life—giving as possible. — Ryan

I want to rise early so I can control the start of my day versus being reactive to the inputs around me. — Steven

Because I want to make a difference with my life and being selfish at 5 a.m. (mentally, physically, and spiritually) puts me in a place where I can give myself away for the rest of the day. — Matt

I want to get things done, plus I want to spend more quality time with the wife. — Lee

My number one reason for wanting to get up early is to have time alone. I'm a stay—at—home mom to three little boys. If I don't get up early, I often don't even get a shower, let alone a few minutes to gather my thoughts for the day. — Becky

Because I always have more focused, productive, and exciting days when I do. I get far more accomplished, and find a greater satisfaction and fulfillment. — Nathan

WHERE DO YOU FIND THE TIME TO RISE EARLY?

Have you ever said any of the following?
I didn't get enough sleep.
I don't have enough time to write a book.
I don't have enough time with my kids.
I haven't been on a date with my wife in a while.
I haven't walked my dog lately..
I need to make more money.
I'm too busy to read.
I don't have enough time to come up with new creative ideas.

You may not have uttered all of those, but you've said some of them. You want more time, but you don't have it. Reason number one is you waste a lot of time. I can hear what you are thinking, and you are disagreeing with me.

You're thinking, "I've got kids. I run a business. I volunteer. My kids are in band, play softball, are on the dance team, and just joined the Lego League." Okay, I get it — you're busy. How many people do you know who say they're not busy? Your goal isn't to be busy. In fact, this experience will make you less busy, because you'll manage your time better and have a better life as a result.

If you're wasting time, you can reclaim that time, go to bed earlier, and then get up earlier. Being early to rise is not about getting less sleep (usually). It's about using your time more wisely.

Find the time to rise early.
Here are three very simple areas in which you can find time so you can start to rise early. Each will require change in your life. Change is hard, but change in order to have a better life is a good thing. Embrace these changes; you'll be glad you did. Here are the three areas:
1. Turn off the screen.
2. Quit some stuff.
3. Sleep less.

Turn off the screen.
I love television, and I'm not alone. The average American watches thirty-four hours of television every week — and that's just TV. Americans also average twenty-one hours each week on social media. Throw in online shopping and reading, and we spend a stupid amount of time in front of a screen. If you work forty hours a week, you're normal. If you spend fifty-five hours in front of a screen, you're also normal. Being normal is not going to help your life get better. You could be doing something else — something truly productive — with those hours.

When our family had a dual-tuner DVR, we could watch one show while recording two others. We could watch a show and still be getting "behind" on our shows at the same time. What a black hole of mindless entertainment! Okay, it wasn't all mindless entertainment, and therein lies another problem. Not all screen time is bad. There are plenty of educational, enriching shows and beneficial blogs and websites. You have to search hard, but you can watch good television.

Leno Words w/ Friends
Mindless TV
Softball League
Email Addiction

QUIT
SOME Stuff

A television is not the box the devil lives in and social media isn't evil, but you need to consume less of it. How?

Option A: Quit cold turkey.

Unplug the cable from the back of your television and put the remotes in the trunk of your car. For the next week, you'll instinctively look for the remote when walking into the room, but then you'll remember it's in the trunk of your car. It's in the trunk because it takes a lot of work to get something out of your trunk instead of just looking in a drawer. If you have a contract with a cable or satellite company, you can usually put your subscription on pause for a period of time for a small monthly fee. This will seem like a pain, and it will take work because it is not normal. It is counter-cultural. That's the point. I don't want to go where culture wants to take me, and neither do you. You could also just call and cancel your service. It's up to you, of course.

Option B: Pick a few shows and websites.

My wife and I watch two shows faithfully. Other than the one show we watch together and the one show I watch by myself (which I watch online), we do our best to not watch television. We're not religious about this, but we've basically decided what few shows we will watch regularly. This is enough for us to keep our television, but it stops us from turning it on every time we're in the living room. In the U.S., it's stunningly common for people to turn on their televisions instead of leaving it off and talking to each other, reading a book, or playing with their kids. Likewise, narrow down your daily website visits, and choose just a few that actually benefit you. Leave the rest behind for a while — they'll still be there when you really need to check them.

Option C: Create a time limit.
Budget how much time you're going to watch television and spend online per week. If you track how many minutes a screen has your attention, you'll be shocked. Cut that time in half, and make it your time limit for the first week of your screen diet. If you spend fifteen hours now, then next week allow yourself seven-and-a-half hours. It may help to choose shows the whole family can watch so you can at least be together during your television time. (Good luck finding a show your whole family can watch together, but if you find a few, that's great.) The next week, try to cut your time in half again. You can still watch and surf, but you need to set a boundary.

Option D: Ditch cable.
This is something my family has done, and it helped cut our television time. We have a ROKU box that allows us to access Netflix, Amazon Prime, and HULU Plus. The small box also allows us to listen to music on Pandora or even watch movies we've loaded on a USB thumb drive, which plugs into the ROKU. In addition, we purchased a high-definition antenna for less than twenty dollars to get our local channels. Our monthly television bill is eight dollars for Netflix. We don't get hundreds of channels, and we love it that way. We don't have to resist what isn't tempting us. Ditch cable, dish, or whatever means by which you're getting hundreds of channels you don't need — and likely aren't watching — on a regular basis. You will miss them for a while, and then you won't.

2. Quit some stuff.
You need to crop your life. Some people believe Americans are lazy, but I believe the opposite. We are very busy. We're

very busy doing the wrong things.

Allow me to sound like an old man. When I was a child, I played basketball, football, and baseball. I played all three sports every year from about age eight until I was in high school. The seasons didn't overlap that much, so it wasn't a problem. I was in Cub Scouts, I was active at my church, and I went on vacations with my family. We did a lot of stuff, but I also played with my brother and friends in my neighborhood a lot. My life was well-balanced because adults in my life built sport seasons that didn't overlap and my parents protected me from doing too many things. Sport seasons for children are too long. Kids are doing too much, and if you're a parent, it's your job to help them organize and prioritize their time. You need to help them say "No" and you will likely have to say "No" to a few adults in the process. Parents must protect their children, and protecting their schedules is a key part.

Children aren't the only busy ones; adults are doing too much as well. If you are doing too much, you're likely driven by one or perhaps both of these negative emotions — guilt or restlessness. If you feel guilty for not doing enough, then you're probably giving more to others than you are caring for yourself. Your family may suffer from your volunteering when you could be home with them. Your kids may suffer because you work too many hours. You may be volunteering at something wonderful, but many people volunteer out of guilt instead of joy and gratitude.

If you do too much, it's also likely you're doing so because of restlessness. If you sit in silence for the next five minutes, your brain will start to do very strange things. We do not know how to sit still. We don't know how to stop and think, so we don't. We just keep going. This book and process will help you learn how to slow down and embrace a routine that bears fruit in your life. If you drive your car at 100 mph for three hours, it will break. Likewise, if you run too fast for too long, you will either become empty or break. We need breaks to care for ourselves, and that's not because we're lazy.

Hamsters on a wheel are very busy. They are restlessly pursuing the next step and going nowhere fast. You're a hamster on a wheel unless you're doing the right things. The Early to Rise process will teach you how to do the right things so your activity creates something healthy over time. No more wasting time on the wrong things. Get off the wheel, and start doing things that get you somewhere in life. This means you may have to quit some things. You will feel guilty, but you'll get over it. Your time is limited, so you need to put limits on your commitments. Restlessness can only be satisfied by meaningful activity.

3. Sleep less.

The best way to find out how much sleep you need is to decrease amount of sleep you get until you don't function well. Then add thirty minutes back to your sleep schedule, and see if that helps. Experiment with your sleep until you find the minimum amount needed for you to still function well. It might be less (or more) sleep than you're currently getting. It's important to get good sleep, so make sure to read something encouraging before bed instead of watching television or checking email. Doing stimulating things before bed isn't healthy for sleep. There are also apps that track how well you sleep and wake you during your more shallow sleep periods. I use an app called Sleep Cycle which tracks my movements while I sleep. It's surprisingly effective at waking me at a time when it's easier for me to wake up. Not bad for ninety-nine cents. EarlyToRiseBook.com/SleepCycle

If you can't sleep less, the next step is to go to bed earlier. Our family starts our bedtime routine around 6:30 p.m. because our kids are very young. I'm often in my pajamas by eight o'clock. If you want to get up early, you need to sleep less or go to bed earlier. It's pretty simple but difficult to do.

WHAT TO DO WHEN YOU GET UP EARLY

Waking up can be dangerous if we're not prepared for it, but we can rise early with consistency and excitement if we're aware of our morning temptations and how to counteract them.

The temptation to start "doing"
When we wake, everything we need to do comes running at us. It attacks us. It attacks the part of our minds that hold peace and clarity. The tasks of our days are aggressive, and they're constantly reminding us just how important they are. If we don't have a plan for our early mornings, then we'll just start worrying earlier than usual. We need to set aside our morning time to just "be" instead of "do."

Voices in the morning
Your television will tell you to watch it. Your phone will tell you there are unanswered emails. (After you read the day's Early to Rise email, turn your phone off. All your friends are asleep.) Your house will tell you to clean, sort, or work on something. We are surrounded by voices telling us to do anything other than take care of ourselves. We must go into a dark hole and hide there with a book and something to write. We have to quiet ourselves with a tool in one hand and something to create in our mind's eye. We must create time intentionally just as we might create a sentence or a piece of art. We must cast

aside that of lesser worth (the day's to-do list and busywork) and feed ourselves so we can in turn feed others.

I have two suggestions for using your early mornings powerfully and wisely. You may not choose to do these two things, but if you do, now is a great time to start.

1. Shut the world out.
It is very important that upon waking you do not engage with the world for at least an hour. You must hold it at bay. Don't check your email other than to read or listen to each day's passage. Don't read or watch the news. Don't text. Don't look through your DVR. Don't listen to anything that causes you to worry. Early morning is a time to fill yourself up, not stress yourself out.

As I write this, a man recently killed twenty children at a Connecticut elementary school. It will be on the news this morning. I'd like to know more about what happened, but I will resist the urge to turn on my television. I have the rest of the day to worry about things I can't control. In the morning, I focus on my story and stories I want to tell. I focus on stories I want to know more about, instead of stories the news chooses to tell me.

If you could choose the stories you hear and see and experience, wouldn't you? Great news: you get to choose most of the stories you experience. If you live in the free world, you have tremendous power to choose your stories. You can choose what books to read and what to do with your time. You can choose where you work and where you live. Sometimes we forget we have choices, but forgetting does not take those choices away. We simply need to wake up! Wake up and realize we don't need to know yet what happened in the world last night. You need to focus on encouraging and empowering stories, and if you have it in you, craft your own stories as well.

2. Create.

My brother is an artist. He went to art school; his work has been displayed and bought. He acts like artists are supposed to act. (You can think whatever you want about that last statement.) I used to think the artist role was taken in my family. If my family was a cast of actors for a play, my brother would play the artist, and he should because he's very talented. In the last few years, I've discovered that I too am an artist.

Guess what? You are an artist too.

Art is anything you create that has your fingerprints on it and gets shared with the world. You can artfully negotiate a sale, artfully create a computer program, or artfully write a non-fiction book about how getting up early can improve life (hypothetically speaking, of course). It's all art. My four-and-a-half year old son is better at drawing than I am. I'm not kidding — he's better than I am. My gifts are mostly focused on speaking and communicating. I'm good with analogies, conversation, and asking great questions. Unfortunately, some of us have had the art sucked out of us, and we need to put it back. We need to reclaim our titles as artists and create something — not for the world, but for our own survival. We need to create for our souls to be healthy and because the world needs what we have locked inside of us.

Mornings are perfect times to search for creative outlets. We can tap away on a keyboard, chip away at wood, doodle, build logos on our computers, write a song, or knit — something that allows us to disengage our self-judgment.

It is vitally important to begin the day with something that is both an outlet and a source of encouragement. Art does

both of those things. Let yourself try things. Most of my words will never be seen by anyone else, but I'm learning to love writing. I go where I feel like going in my heart and head, and it works. Where does your head and heart need to go to feel healthy? Your mornings will become the time for you to go there.

A morning routine

I don't expect your routine to be the same as mine because mine isn't a routine. It's a buffet of choices. You can make your own menu, and then choose from that menu each day.

Read.

Reading is the conversation between a reader and words on the page. Words are at the mercy of the reader's reaction, imagination, and perception. Reading is a wonderful way to have a conversation about one topic for a long period of time.

For me, reading is like walking around a sculpture to see its many different angles and nuances. Reading helps me appreciate every part of a story, topic, or person. It's good for my mind and my soul. I encourage you to read books that bring you life and joy, not books that cause you worry or guilt. Save those for another time. Morning is the time to set direction for the rest of the day. What you read must put you in the right frame of mind and set a tone for what you're going to experience over the next sixteen or more hours.

Read books you are able to put down and pick up later. When one of my kids wakes up at six-thirty in the morning, I need to be interruptible. Interruptions aren't preferred, but that's life. Sometimes we need to be available even when we don't feel like it. Welcome to adulthood.

Write.

If you've ever desired to be a writer, mornings are the perfect time to satisfy that desire. If you are using a computer, find software that provides a distraction-free window. I use a program called ByWord, but there are others such as OmmWriter or the default text editor, TextEdit. The point is to remove any distractions from what is most important: getting words on a page. If you'd like to write a book, consider buying a program called Scrivener (EarlyToRiseBook.com/Scrivener). Scrivener makes writing a book easier than you can imagine.

Set a goal to write a certain number of words every day. My goal is one thousand words a day, and it takes me about thirty minutes if I'm focused. If I'm doing true free-writing — as taught by Mark Levy in his book *The Accidental Genius* (EarlyToRiseBook.com/AccidentalGenius) — I write even faster. Setting a goal and reaching it creates a feeling of success in the morning. The goal is not one thousand great words; it's one thousand words. Both ByWord and Scrivener have the option to display a running word count at the bottom of the page, which is a great feature to help with reaching the goal.

Listen.

I hate listening (just ask my wife). In one sense, listening is so powerless, but it is also fascinating and profound because it requires our full attention. Half listening is not listening. True listening requires our all. In the morning, listen for your fears and address them. Listen to the things trying to force their way into your heart and mind, and instead of letting them in, view them objectively and have a conversation with yourself about them. Do this silently and attentively — you are listening.

Once a day, make **1 DECISION** that will **CHANGE** one **PERSON FOREVER**

That day is *today*.

That decision is to get out of bed *early*.

That person is *you*.

A SIMPLE REMINDER

Once a day, make one decision that will change one person forever.

That day is today.
That decision is to get out of bed early.
That person is you.

REMINDER: GET THE BONUS CONTENT!

There was already a whole page about this, but I want to remind you again of by far the most powerful thing you can do to build your habit. Sign up for the daily emails and get the audio verson of the book for free.

By purchasing this book, you are entitled to receive the full audio edition, as well as thirty days of email encouragement to help you succeed in building your Early to Rise habit.

Each day is emailed to you every morning around 2 a.m. CT along with a link to listen to me read that day's passage. The content of the emails is the same as the content of the book. This is a great way to build your habit, and most readers find it to be the key to learning their habit of rising early.

To redeem bonuses, visit EarlyToRiseBook.com/Extras.

Important Notes:
>> Accountability emails: If you sign up for the email accountability program after 8 p.m. CDT, you may need to wait an extra day to receive the first daily email.
>> There is no way to change the order of the emails you are receiving if you get behind.
>> If you want to sign up to get the thirty days of emails again, simply use a new email address and sign up again.

If you have any trouble getting your bonuses, reach out at EarlyToRiseBook.com/Contact.

THE EXPERIENCE

DAY ONE

Believe and Stand Up

As you begin this experience, I am inviting you to believe in yourself. It may feel silly, but take a moment to imagine how your life will change because of your daily decision to rise early. Imagine how much more peace you will have as you start the day. Imagine greeting your family every morning with kind and encouraging words. Imagine writing a book this year. Imagine a different life than you have now.

If you want to fix your life, you are in a great place. You can do it if you believe and take the time to make the necessary changes. The first change you need to make is your mindset.

Your mindset matters. Mindset becomes momentum, and momentum brings change. Sportscasters talk about a game's momentum moving in one team's favor, but no one can see momentum. You can feel momentum, and you can see its effects. If you have the proper mindset for one minute a day over the next thirty days, you will change your life forever. One minute a day is what it takes for you to turn off your alarm, put your feet on the floor, put on some slippers, and walk out of your bedroom.

You will change your family tree. You will accomplish more in one morning than you've achieved in the last ten mornings. You will have more joy as you go through your day. You will be a better spouse, parent, student, leader, and employee. This will all happen through a small window of time you create every single day for the next thirty days.

The key to success in this challenge is simple: take action when the window is open. Every day your alarm will sound, and you will have two options — you can either wake up or stay asleep. It takes one minute to make that decision. From the moment you hear the alarm, you will start to wake. You will either put your feet on the floor and stand, or you will keep them in your bed.

A friend of mine had a condition caused by fear and mental illness which kept her from getting out of bed. She prayed for God to tell her what He wanted her to do to overcome her illness, and God told her to make her bed.

Get out of bed. You will change your life by rising early.

She knew (and He knew, of course) if she made her bed, she would not climb back into it. She made her bed that day, and she made her bed again the next day. She defeated her illness by listening to God when He told her to make her bed.

I'm not God, but I'm telling you the same thing. Get out of bed. You *will* change your life by rising early. You will change your life if you put your feet on the floor and push, also known as standing.

A few more thoughts on mindset:
Expect success every single day of this challenge.
Expect new ideas.
Expect personal growth.
Expect a new perspective.
Expect you might need to use two alarms tomorrow.

ACTION TIP:
Choose a spot where you can sit for more than an hour. You should find a cozy and quiet spot that allows you to maintain good posture. Set out everything you need tonight for your early morning time, so you are looking forward to settling into your spot when you wake up tomorrow. Set the stage for a successful morning.

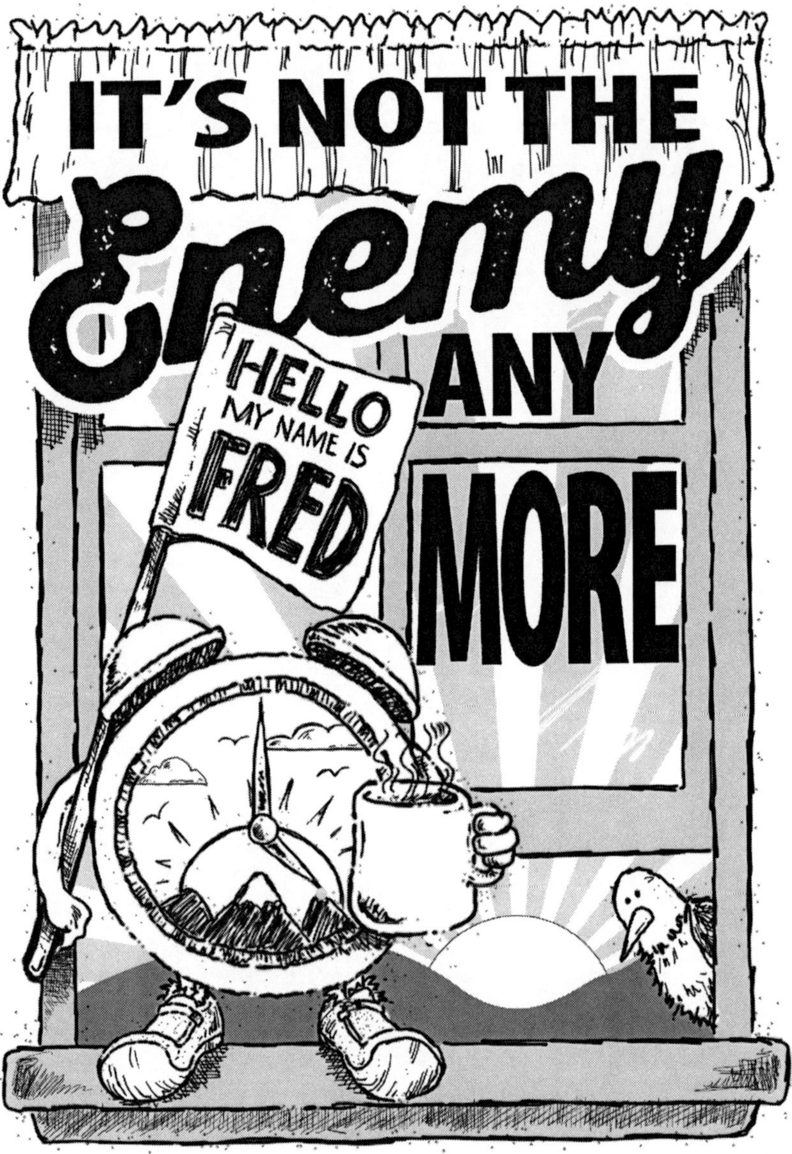
IT'S NOT THE
Enemy
ANY
MORE
HELLO
MY NAME IS
FRED

It's Not the Enemy Anymore

First, congratulations on rising early today. If you're reading this as part of your morning ritual, then you are awesome — even though you have bed-head and your breath stinks.

It's time for you to meet your new friend. Until today you have always thought of him as your enemy. He is your alarm clock. Whether an app on your phone or old-school ringing bells that shake on the nightstand, your alarm is going to help change your life for the better. It has one job, and that job is to help you. Don't hate your alarm.

You need to name your alarm clock. I suggest you name him Fred. You can hate a machine jolting you from your comfort, but would you hate a friend who woke you up to get a head start on an adventure? Your day is an adventure, and Fred will help you start it.

Tomorrow morning, you will have a choice how to think:

» Either, the alarm clock is my enemy. It opposes my peace; therefore, I hate it. When it speaks, I will despise it.

» Or, Fred is my friend. He wants me to have a better life, so he's going to get my lazy butt out of bed now. He tells me when I can start another great day full of opportunities to improve myself, my family, and the world. I love Fred because Fred loves me. Fred is the first person I see every day, and he does his job well. Fred has my back. Fred is on the adventure with me.

Tomorrow morning, greet Fred. Say, "Good morning, my friend! You are annoying, but I appreciate it. Fred, you've done your job well because I'm talking to you, which means I'm awake." You might just cuss at Fred, but that's okay. He can take it; he's an alarm clock. He's used to being yelled at.

ACTION TIP:

Talk to Fred every day. Buy an alarm clock, or download the Sleep Cycle app: EarlyToRiseBook.com/SleepCycle. It tracks your sleep patterns and will wake you during your shallow sleep, which makes it easier to wake up. You have to give it a thirty-minute window to wake up, so you won't likely wake up at the same time every day. You will usually wake up more refreshed though, because you won't wake up from the deepest part of your sleep. I love the Rise app — EarlyToRiseBook.com/RiseAlarm — because it's very easy to adjust, has a great user interface, and includes really good alarm sounds.

DAY THREE

Are You Being Selfish?

When I find out someone I know is going to have a baby, I do what everyone does: I offer some free, unsolicited advice. I tell them not to compare their life before the baby with their life after the baby. Having a baby doesn't just change life; it completely resets life. Everything is different. Babies need you all the time!

How do we balance children's needs and getting up early? Having kids and getting up early might seem like opposing forces, but they're not. Actually, the key to having a great day while raising kids is getting up early. Kids or no kids, there is no time left for you to do what you want to do between 7 a.m. and 10 p.m. If there was, you wouldn't be reading this book. You would be content, and your life would be skipping along nicely. You want more, and the only time you are going to get it is early in the morning.

As my friend Jon Acuff says, you need to "be selfish at 5 a.m." Waking up early gives you a chance to focus on your goals, your dreams, your inner-life. You need to be selfish with that time and spend it on yourself. Jon got a job working for Dave Ramsey because he was selfish at 5 a.m. for several years. He hustled and built his business early in the morning while working a full-time job during the day and being a good husband and father to two girls.

When you're selfish, just make sure it doesn't mess up everyone else's schedule or take time away from them. If you want to pursue your dream, go for it. If you want to write or knit or build or read, go for it! But do it on your time.

If you are afraid to be selfish by getting up early and using the time for yourself, remember it's not bad to be a more disciplined and healthy person. A better you will improve your family, workplace, church, and all your relationships. This challenge will make you a better person because you're taking control of your life by taking control of your mornings.

By the way, how is Fred doing? I love that guy. Did you two talk this morning?

ACTION TIP:
If you don't have any, buy some house slippers today. Comfort is perhaps the biggest obstacle to getting up early, and slippers make waking up early bearable. Set them by your bed facing out so you can slip into them when you get out of bed (just like the cover of this book). You need to equip yourself for success, and house slippers are part of your arsenal. When your feet hit the floor, they need someplace just as warm and cozy as your bed. Make your feet happy to be out of bed. Slippers are a worthwhile investment.

DAY FOUR

You Are In Control

If you want to end a conversation with me, start talking about the weather. I've lived in four states, and every one of them is full of people who talk about the weather as if they've never experienced it before.

"I hate this snow!" I hear that one a lot in South Dakota, but a South Dakotan hating snow is like a Hawaiian hating sand. Get over it! Or during the summer, "This heat sure is getting old." It's summer! If you'd like a cold front, I hear Canada still has some room for people.

Pardon my sarcasm, but I have no patience for discussing things we can't control. I have a hard enough time keeping control where I can! There are many, many things in life you cannot control. It would do us all good to stop focusing on those things and focus instead on what we can change.

What do you control? You control what time you wake up. You do not control who wakes up five minutes after you do. See proof below from the day I wrote this chapter:

MY LITTLE BUDDY (AND MY DOG)

How do we focus on the things we can control? Run away from the things you can't control. Here's how:

> » Read or listen to something encouraging before you go to sleep. Don't watch television right before you go to bed, especially the news.
> » Go to bed early. You may need eight hours of sleep, or you may need six. The quickest way to fail to rise early is to go to bed too late.
> » Be nice to Fred. He's your alarm clock, and he's your friend. Welcome him.
> » Put your feet on the floor in the first ten seconds. Don't miss the window of opportunity. Don't think about how your head feels when you wake up. Move your feet, and get them on the ground and into those new slippers.
> » Have something planned. Have the coffee made and a book waiting for you in a comfortable chair. Have something to look forward to.

When you choose to wake early, you set the tone for the rest of your day. You begin from a position of control. You direct the day instead of it shaking you from your lazy sleep. Take control of your day because days become weeks, weeks become months, and months become years. Years make a life, and you only get one.

ACTION TIP:
Pick a song to listen to or a book to read before you go to bed tonight so you can fall asleep with good thoughts on your mind. In the absence of good input, we allow negative thoughts and worry to enter our minds. Find something encouraging to listen to or read, and keep it by your bed. Don't go to sleep without spending at least a few minutes consuming goodness so you can sleep better.

Challenge

You've started a **challenge**. Here are three definitions of what you're going through:

1. **A call to take part in a contest or competition, esp. a duel: he accepted the *challenge*.** You signed up for this. You've accepted the challenge, and I congratulate you for that. Remember that this is a duel — it's you against one decision every day: sleep or rise early.

2. **A task or situation that tests someone's abilities: the ridge is a *challenge* for experienced climbers.** Do you have any idea what you are capable of? Probably not. This will test your abilities, and in doing so, it will make you stronger. You're going to improve.

3. **An attempt to win a contest or championship in a sport: a world title *challenge*.** Every morning is a contest for you, and every day you have a chance at victory.

> *If getting up early was easy, you would already be doing it.*

This experience is not called Early To Rise Because It's Easy. This is the Thirty-Day Early To Rise *Challenge*. If getting up early was easy, you would already be doing it, and you would know lots of others doing it too. Be proud of yourself — you are taking a challenge. Some days the challenge will win, but most days you will. This contest will test your abilities and end with a winner and a loser. I believe you're going to win. Do you?

ACTION TIP:
If you drink coffee in the morning, drink it black for a few days. Don't do it because it tastes better, because it might not. Do it because you need to get out of your routines. Show yourself you can change. I was a cream-and-sugar guy for a long time, but drinking coffee black has really grown on me, and I enjoy it more now. If you don't drink coffee, God bless you. I have no idea how you function in the morning, but keep it up.

Adjust Your Attitude

Actions change your attitude, and your attitude is changing. If someone told you a week ago that he or she got up at the time you did today, you would have said, "There's no way I can do that!" Now you're doing it. Your attitude is changing because your actions are different.

My son woke up at 6:15 this morning, and now he is sitting next to me playing a snowball game on my iPad. It reminded me of the first week I took this challenge for myself a year ago. It was a horrible experience until I changed my attitude.

My goal was to wake up an hour before my kids got up. The "problem" came every morning fifteen minutes after I woke up. No matter what time I got up, my kids woke up fifteen minutes after me. Instead of greeting them warmly, I felt interrupted and would try to force them to go back to sleep. For what it's worth, that doesn't work.

When I shifted my attitude, I realized I had been ignoring a gift. If my children woke up early every once in a while, I could spend more time than ever with them, and I still got to work on time. I'm grateful when they sleep in, but now I also embrace interruptions.

> *There are no referees. Do what works for you, and be sure to enjoy the process.*

This is a challenge, but there are no referees. Do what works for you, and be sure to enjoy the process.

ACTION TIP:
If your mornings are interrupted regularly by other people, explain to them the importance of your alone time. If it is your kids, have books for them to read or download some educational apps for them to play on your phone or iPad. If your spouse interrupts you, explain to him or her that you need some alone time.

DAY SEVEN

Brick by Brick

There are different opinions on exactly how many days it takes to build a habit, as evidenced by an article titled *How Long Does it Take an Action to Become a Habit; 21, 28, or 66 Days?* by Kathryn Goetzke from PsychCentral.com. You'll be encouraged to know that when you form a habit but then break it, it's possible to pick it up very easily because our physical brain has changed to wire us to continue the habit. Goetzke sites research from the UK Health Behaviore Research Centre which found habits take up to sixty-six days to form. No matter how many days it takes to form your habit, remember the following: the only number that matters in building this habit is "one".

> » Habits happen **one** decision at a time.
> » Habits die **one** decision at a time.
> » Habits start **one** day.
> » Habits are the responsibility of **one** person.
> » Habits are formed by people who realize they only get **one** life.
> » Habits are formed by the **one** person you can control: you.

The Early To Rise Experience is optional. There is no financial penalty for sleeping in. I won't show up on your doorstep tomorrow at whatever time you are supposed to wake up. I'm not your mom or your dad (unless your name is Samuel, Caroline, or Lucy and you live in my house), so I'm not going to storm into your bedroom if you hit snooze twenty-eight times.

People from all over the world have told me this experience changed their life. This is about taking responsibility for your life. Your life. Your morning. Your friend Fred. It's all *yours*. What are you going to do with it?

ACTION TIP:
Download the Lift app (Lift.do) and add some habits to start tracking. Most importantly, make sure to add some easier habits in order to help you build more difficult ones. It is proven to help if you have easy and difficult habits mixed together. As of this book's publication, Lift was only available for iOS devices but should be coming to other platforms soon.

Ship Something

You are an artist even though you probably don't think of yourself as one. Art comes in many forms. View what you create as art, because it is unique and beautiful. The way you listen to others can be your art. The way you speak can be your art. The way my wife deals with our kids while I'm at work is art. How I create podcasts or write books is art. You have art in you as well, and art is beautiful.

Rising early is giving you more time to create and hone your art, and the world is a better place when it has more of your art in it. Today, add your art. Ship something. Seth Godin uses the term "shipping" to refer to creating something and getting it out into the world. It's not enough to make something; you are not shipping until you put it out into the world. Shipping is like being married or pregnant — you either are or you aren't.

Ship something because most people spend most of their lives consuming. You don't want to be like most people, so take the risk of becoming a creator instead of just a consumer. When you ship something you're creating it and putting it into the world. Birth something today. Giving life to something else will give you life.

Putting art out into the world is difficult and vulnerable, but the world needs more great books, songs, drawings, paintings, and other forms of art. Here are some things you could create and ship:

» Write a letter to a friend.

- » Build a LEGO-city with your kids.
- » Knit a hat to donate to charity.
- » Draw a picture and post it on your blog.
- » Plant a garden with your neighbors.
- » Bake cookies for some firefighters, librarians, teachers, or favorite author. (I really like oatmeal raisin. Thanks.)
- » Buy flowers, help the florist arrange the bouquet, and give them to your wife. Get a note from the florist stating you "helped". She'll like that part.
- » Start the book you've always wanted to write. (Writing 500 words each day for two months makes a 120-page book.)

For seven days, you've been prodded, encouraged, and nudged, but now it is time to ship something. I would love to know what you shipped. Visit http://www.EarlyToRiseBook.com/contact and let me know. I want to be the first to say, "Congratulations."

ACTION TIP:
Make a goal to build your art over the next few weeks. Give yourself daily goals that result in a larger goal being met. Create a timeline with specific action steps and benchmarks. Then, ship it!

The Spirit of the Challenge

I remember failing to rise early on my ninth day of this challenge. My two oldest kids were sick, and I sat in bed propping them up so they wouldn't cough because their lungs were full of phlegm. I didn't rise early to pour into me; I stayed in bed to pour into them. If rising early was about checking a box every day, then that day was a failure. This challenge isn't about check boxes though — it's about changing your life.

» The goal isn't to rise early so you can brag on Twitter. (Use #EarlyToRise if you do want to brag though.)

» The goal isn't to feel better than other people.

» The goal isn't to read more books or pray more prayers.

» The goal is a better you.

Rising early will make you a better person. Rising early will change your life and the lives of those around you. If you happen to not get up on time every morning, then so be it. The world will not stop spinning because your kids needed you to snuggle with them or because you were just lazy for a day. The spirit of this challenge is to improve yourself so you can improve the world, which starts with your impact on your family and goes out from there.

Take this experience seriously, but don't be legalistic. Plans are wonderful things, but reality is often different. Accept reality, and try again tomorrow.

If you feel alone in this challenge, head over to Twitter.

com and search for #EarlyToRise. You'll find other people who are taking the challenge. Connect with them, and encourage each other. You can also find more Early To Rise success stories and advice at EarlyToRiseBook.com. Just remember that you're not alone. Ever.

ACTION TIP:
If you only had fifteen minutes of time for yourself each morning, what is the one thing you would do during that time? Some days, you won't have your full morning time because your kids need attention, you have to go to work early, or you just plain slept in. Decide to do something every day that gives you life, even if you only have fifteen minutes to do it. Do that one thing right now. If you have more than fifteen minutes, great. If not, aren't you glad you are doing today's action step?

DAY TEN

Your Best Hours

For most of us, the first three hours of the day are our best for thinking in new and unique ways. Our minds are refreshed, and our bodies are rested. Your ideas are up at 5 a.m., but until now you've been asleep, so you missed them. Your ideas need you to listen to them. If you wake up feeling behind and rushed, there's no hope for you to spend time with your ideas and listen to them, let alone take action on them.

If you were like me before you started this challenge, your day started sometime between 7:00 and 9:00 a.m.

> 7:00 – Wake up to unhappy children
>
> 7:05 – Drag myself out of bed and downstairs to let dog out and start coffee
>
> 7:10–8:00 – Blur of activity until I arrive at work.

If you've adjusted your schedule, your mornings could look like this.

> 5:00 – Fred wakes me up (I love that guy!), and my feet hit the floor.
>
> 5:08 – Dog has food and has taken care of business outside. I have a cup of coffee and am sitting in my living room.
>
> 5:08–7:00 – Read, write, listen, pray.
>
> 7:00 – Greet my crabby or happy kids with a big smile and a word of encouragement as they come downstairs

7:02–7:10 – Snuggle with kids

7:10–8:00 – Hand kids iPad, take a shower, get dressed, convince kids to give the iPad back, feed kids, and head to work.

Your clarity is stronger at certain times of the day. For proof of this, try to start an important work task at 4:30 p.m. It's not gonna happen. I think very clearly at 5:10 a.m. I do not think very clearly at five o'clock, but give me ten minutes and I'm ready to change the world.

Your ideas will be up dark and early tomorrow. (It's not that bright at 5 a.m.) Be there to greet them.

ACTION TIP:

Eat something that gives you energy in the morning. Fruit is great; cereal is not. There's no point waking up early and ruining it with food that keeps you from feeling great.

Change the World

Has someone ever told you the impact you've had on their life and you've been surprised? You hadn't realized the effect you had on them. It's time to stop being surprised. It's time to believe you're going to change the world, and that begins with helping people. It's time to start.

You've gotten out of bed early, and you are going to create something important with your time. You are going to have a great attitude at work today because you're mentally prepared for the challenges of the meetings, customers, students, patients, and coworkers who greet you. You are going to be an optimistic person who talks to anyone because your attitude isn't going to change.

When you take care of yourself at the start of your day, you can spend the rest of the day pouring into others.

You are pouring into yourself today, so now you are pouring into others through encouragement. You are going to be thankful for little things with those you know — "Thanks for getting the kids dressed this morning!" And with those you don't know — "You're a great waiter. Thanks for the great service today."

If you don't rise early, you are more likely to be rude to your spouse and short with your kids, drive to work like a jerk, and be impatient with everyone around you. When you take care of yourself at the start of your day, you can spend the rest of the day pouring into others. That sounds like a pretty awesome world, doesn't it?

It's your world, so change it.

ACTION TIP:

Take some cash out of your wallet or purse, Keep it handy in your pocket today, and look for a way to spend it on someone else. Buy a stranger's coffee, treat your kids to something special, or buy your wife a rose.

Do Not Go With the Flow

I hate the term "go with the flow." If you're going with the flow, you're likely normal, average, and not that happy about life. Perhaps I'm being pessimistic, but aren't most people either anxious and worried or resigned that their situation will never improve?

You do not have to go with the flow! Getting up early is getting you out of the flow. If this experience is difficult, it's because you are cutting a new path for your life. You are in control, it's hard work, and no one else can do the work for you.

> *You do not have to go with the flow! Getting up early is getting you out of the flow.*

It's very important to understand what you're up against. "The flow" is happening all around you, and you need to pay attention to it. Find a setting today where people are busy: a lunchroom, restaurant, subway station, sidewalk, or intersection. Watch the people. Look at how busy they are. They're talking, walking, eating, and driving in some combination. Look how frazzled they seem.

Do you see peace on their faces? Is anyone really enjoying the journey? I'm not saying you have to walk twice as slow as everyone else, but would it be so bad if you did?

Being busy is first a frame of mind; our bodies follow suit. You choose to plan or not plan. You choose to leave on time or not leave on time. You choose to say yes or no to commitments.

If you are going with the flow, guess who's in control? The flow is. Pay attention to the craziness, and then choose a different way of life. Going with the flow may just lead you over a waterfall.

ACTION TIP:

Write down everything you have to do today, then write it again but insert three fifteen minute breaks. During those breaks relax, take a walk, take a jog, take a nap, hum a song. Take three fifteen minute breaks, and your day will improve. Our bodies weren't designed to never rest, so don't force yours to stay in constant motion.

DAY THIRTEEN

Bless Somebody

It's healthy to take care of yourself. It's not selfish to be healthy and whole so you can be a better parent, spouse, friend, or employee. At some point though, you will find a morning rhythm, and when you do, I want you to spend time focusing on other people.

Write down one hundred ways you can encourage, bless, or help people in your life. Some of the ones I wrote down include:

- » Empty the dishwasher before my wife wakes up.
- » Write a one-line email to all my clients with specific encouragement on why I appreciate them.
- » Wake my kids up on Saturday and go get donuts.
- » Open a savings account dedicated to buying books for friends, and set up a monthly automatic deposit into the account.

Those are just a few examples of things you can do for others. If you spend a morning coming up with one hundred ideas and execute ten of them, you will change a lot of lives for the better — including yours.

This challenge is about your mindset and development, but you should also spend time blessing others. Life lived for yourself is too small. You can change the world; the key is finding the time to do it.

I will be up at 5 a.m. tomorrow too. Let's both change the world. Bless somebody, and you'll bless yourself in the process.

ACTION TIP:

Write a list of one hundred ways you can bless people around you. They don't have to be good ideas or even reasonable ones. Just write down your ideas. If you'd like, you can email me the list by visiting www.EarlyToRiseBook.com/contact.

Make It Cost Something

When something has a price, people ascribe a value to it. When something is free, recipients are more likely to ignore, forget, or neglect it. If you've been struggling with this challenge, it's time to raise the stakes and put a price on your laziness.

If you had to catch a flight tomorrow at 5 a.m., you would wake up much earlier in order to get ready and get to the airport. If you missed your flight, the penalty would be hundreds of dollars or hours of waiting at the airport. Sometimes penalties are great motivators.

If you're consistently failing to get up early, then do the following;

1. Set out your clothes for the next day before you go to bed. Socks, shoes, everything.
2. Get your cereal bowl ready, or put a skillet on the stove along with the mixing bowl and whisk for the eggs you're going to cook.
3. Do NOT set two alarms.
4. Do not hit the snooze button.
5. Make plans to meet a friend for lunch. Promise your friend you'll buy lunch if you don't send him or her a message within ten minutes of your wake-up time. If you send the message, have lunch but each pay for your own meals. If you don't send the message, have lunch and you pay for both meals.

If I had to find $100,000 in the next twenty-four hours

to save the life of one of my children, I could. Consequences motivate us. If you're struggling to rise early, give yourself some consequences. Make waking up cost you something. Get rid of the excuses: two alarms, a snooze button, and no consequences. You can get up early, and — if it costs you enough — you will get up early.

ACTION TIP:
Tell your spouse if you hit the snooze button, he or she gets to spend $20 at their favorite store that day.

DAY FIFTEEN

Half-Way

Baseball players can get into the Hall of Fame for not hitting the ball sixty-six percent of the time. If they get hits thirty-three percent of the time, they're considered great hitters. How many mornings have you gotten up on time during the first half of this challenge? Don't be hard on yourself if your batting average is thirty-three percent. I really hope it gets better over time, but the only way you can guarantee success is to keep trying.

If the first half of this challenge has been a failure, start over. If you want to restart the emails, simply unsubscribe using the link at the bottom of the emails and then resubscribe. The emails will start over at Day One, and if you woke up on time today, you've got a perfect record! You're doing awesome! You're one-for-one!

We spend far too much time looking at the past and believing it will determine the future.

We spend far too much time looking at the past and believing it will determine the future. For a short time, I worked with investments. On every piece of investment literature I showed customers, there was a very clear disclaimer which said something like, "Past performance is not a guarantee of future performance."

I had to tell customers that disclaimer so they wouldn't expect a mutual fund that went up twenty percent last year to go up twenty percent again this year. It could go down fifty

85

percent! The disclaimer protected us from expectations that were too high.

You need to claim a disclaimer for yourself: *Past (poor) performance is not an indication of future (poor) performance.*

You know who's not perfect? Everybody.

You know who fails? People who try to achieve great things.

You know who gets knocked down by others? People who try to stand up for something.

If something is difficult, that's likely a sign it's important. If you've failed, get over it and win tomorrow. It's a new day.

Past performance is not an indication of future performance.

You're going to do great. Believe that about yourself. I believe it about you.

ACTION TIP:
Create a public place — our group at Lift.do, Facebook, Twitter, Instagram, the office water cooler — to track your Early To Rise success as a reminder of your commitment to the challenge and for public accountability.

DAY SIXTEEN

Stupid Early

Good habits are hard to build, and bad habits are hard to break. Getting up early is a good habit. Going to bed late is a bad habit. There is one indisputable key to getting up early for this challenge: go to bed on time. You have to give up a bad habit in order to gain a good one.

What time should you go to bed? You will figure it out through trial and error. I need to go to bed at ten o'clock — ten-thirty at the latest — if I want to get up at five. When I go to bed at ten-thirty, there is a seventy-five percent chance I will get up at five. When I go to bed at nine-thirty, there is a ninety-five percent chance I will get up at five.

What are you doing the last hour of your day? If you answered "watching television," I've got great news — you just found an extra hour of sleep. Even if you're not tired, climb into bed an hour earlier than usual. Bring a book along, and read for a bit. It's likely you won't miss that hour of television, and it's likely that you'll get up early and start your day on a wonderful note.

If you want to control the starting line of tomorrow morning, get control of the finish line tonight.

If you want to control the starting line of tomorrow morning, get control of the finish line tonight. Set an alarm to tell you what time to get into bed. Ask Fred to help you out. He's really good at reminding you about stuff.

ACTION TIP:

Go to bed stupid early tonight. Go to bed an hour earlier than you usually do. If you feel silly, get over it. Remember to listen to or read something positive before you go to sleep too.

DAY SEVENTEEN

Rest

Americans are obsessed with doing things. We are so obsessed with doing things we are usually doing more than one thing at a time. In your morning time, do not do more than one thing at a time. Don't forget that peace and rest are parts of waking up early.

Everyone is prone to jump from one task to another, but that wandering comes at a cost:

> » Our minds cannot rest.
> » Our tasks lose quality.
> » Our hearts are unsettled.
> » Our loved ones rarely get our full attention.
> » We are unable to consider deeper ideas and larger issues.
> » We cannot hear God when He is trying to speak to us.

The solution to missing out on so much is to do less. That's right — to enjoy more, we must do less. Morning is just the beginning; we must seek to find peace in doing less throughout the day. We can experience rest all day by simplifying our tasks and being present in every moment. This is a shift not just in action but also in thought, so do not expect your mind to obey immediately. Embracing single-tasking is believing that by doing less while focusing more you will achieve more, and that is hard logic to accept. Try it though, and see if I'm right. If it doesn't work, go back to your multi-tasking ways.

Do Not Do More THAN 1 THING AT A TIME

As for the morning, remember it's okay to wake up early and just sit with a cup of coffee or tea. Don't feel the need to "do." There are times to ship and times to rest. If you're obsessed with work, morning can be the time to rest your mind. Change your expectations of yourself. Often, the best thing we can do is simply be.

It is very, very difficult for me to sit and listen because I am so loud, not in my volume but in my busy thoughts. My mind has too many things to consider and not enough capacity to process them all at the same time. Uninterrupted mornings give me the space I need to sort out my thoughts. Imagine a table full of pictures which tell a story. The pictures need to be a certain order to tell the story correctly, and you need a big enough table to put them in order. You need space to make sense of it all. The same is true of your mind. You need space to make sense of your life. While I struggle to be still, I have learned to rest and quiet my mind by doing only one thing at a time. I have space to think and make sense of my day ahead. Give yourself that gift today.

Pause the music to take a sip of coffee.

Don't listen to music while you read.

Use only one computer program at a time. Force yourself to close it before you open another.

Your brain is trained to do several things at once, but it's not good for your mind, body, or spirit. Today, try your best to do one thing at a time, and as you readjust, the result will be an experience of rest.

It is ironic that I'm encouraging you to rest and also get up so early in the morning. Who doesn't want more peace and clarity? Doing less with better focus will result in understanding, seeing, and achieving more.

ACTION TIP:
Download a program called Freedom which blocks a computer from connecting to the Internet for a specific period of time. The only way to get back online is to restart the machine or wait for the time limit to end. The program works for both PC and Mac, and you can find it at MacFreedom.com.

DAY EIGHTEEN

Sum Total

What is the cumulative effect of this challenge? What will happen in your life because you go to bed earlier and wake up earlier? Even you will never know the impact this change will have on the world.

If it is true one person can change the world with evil acts, we also know one person can change the world through kindness. One ignorant person can cause tremendous damage, and one wise person can alter the course of history. One lazy father can bring ruin to his household, and one disciplined father can bring great wisdom, peace, prosperity, and joy to his household.

Every day, we choose who we will be. We can view ourselves as loved and therefore love others, or we can view ourselves as losers unable to earn the love of our Creator and others. We can choose to be agents of peace, or we can choose to deliver criticism, discouragement, and anger. We choose to be wise and moral, or we can choose to be selfish and disgraceful.

Many prominent leaders in our day have made poor decisions — usually involving extramarital sex or getting money without earning it — and have lost their positions, families, and careers as a result. Those poor decisions weren't necessarily difficult decisions though. Poor, easy decisions have the harshest cumulative effects because poor decisions multiply the same way good ones do.

We can choose the easier way, or we can choose a better way. By waking up early, we start the day with a good decision, and as long as we use our time to do healthy things, our days will be better. Life has few heroic moments, but great people are ready for them because they've been making many smaller right decisions. Small decisions handled well give us the potential to make larger right decisions, even under pressure.

You are choosing who you are going to be today. You are not a victim. You are not the economy. You are not an employee or even a citizen. Choose the role you want to fulfill; then fill it. If you believe you are a writer, write. If you believe you are a composer, create music. If you believe you are a handy with a saw, let the sawdust fly.

You already made the great decision to start your day early. Continue to make good small decisions, and the cumulative effect will be a much better life for you and those you encounter throughout your days.

ACTION TIP:
Write down your roles. Mine are father, husband, business owner, friend, church member, writer, citizen, son, and brother. After you've written that list, circle two roles in which you want to excel today. Do what it takes today to be better in those roles.

DAY NINETEEN

Tell Today What To Do

Unless the good Lord calls you home today, you will be awake for fifteen to nineteen hours. What is your plan for today? Will you work or watch a movie later? Will you cut the grass or take your wife out on a date? You will do something today, so take a few minutes after today's passage, and write down your schedule. Don't plan it down to the minute, and don't write a to-do list. Write down when you are going somewhere and what you're going to do there. Here's mine:

    5:00 a.m. ..... Wake up, read, write, relax

    7:00 a.m. ..... Feed the kids, then get myself ready

    7:30 a.m. ..... Help Sara with kids

    8:00 a.m. ..... Work: write, record podcasts, etc.

    Noon .... Lunch by myself, read marriage book by Davis

    1:00 p.m. ..... Work: social media, new post, planning for 2013

    4:00 p.m. ..... Home and play with kids

    7:00 p.m. ..... Kids upstairs for bed

    8:00 p.m. ..... Talk with Sara about whatever she wants to talk about, surf net, watch TV

    10:00 p.m. ... Read marriage book by Davis, go to bed

When you look ahead, you are in control. You didn't wake up early by accident, and you don't need to walk through your day by accident. You may not be self-employed and have lots of available time like I do to choose your schedule, but you should have some available time. If you don't have time for yourself or if all your time is for yourself, reprioritize. Look ahead, and control your day as much as you can. You are not a victim of your day.

Victim thinking convinces us that life just happens, and there's nothing we can do about it. Victims have no control over their days, so they throw their hands up and hope for the best. Responsible, empowered thinking allows us to live with purpose and take responsibility for what happens to us. If one is nature, the other is nurture. Victim thinking says your day is a product of your environment (nature), but empowered thinking says your day is what you make it (nurture). You are not a victim of your day. You are in control.

You woke up early today, so you've already shown how much control you can have over your circumstances. Keep it up throughout the day. It's your day, so make it a great one.

ACTION TIP:
Write out your schedule, and look for places to be more productive and places you need to rest. If you find sections of time that seem very large considering the tasks you need to do inside them, you're probably wasting time during that section. Fix it.

Stop Talking

Silence isn't easily found. It must be searched for or created. Stop and listen. What do you hear right now?

I am at a coffee shop. From my chair, I can hear three conversations, jazzy Christmas music, a heater above the door to keep the cold air out, change hitting the drawer in the cash register, and of course, the sound of machines grinding, steaming, and dispensing coffee. Where do I find silence here? I have to create it. I found silence by putting in headphones and playing instrumental music. My surroundings faded to the background like a canvas does for a painting.

Silence is elusive. It hides in small rooms and wide-open spaces, but in our day-to-day lives, it is nearly impossible to find. Silence is like a great marriage: it never just happens, you have to create it. Hopefully, your morning time has some silence built into it.

Silence can actually be difficult to enjoy when we first

experience it. Silence is so rare that, when discovered, it becomes a different kind of noise. When we experience silence, we usually end it. Get in your car, and listen. It's likely silent in your car, and your habit is to turn on the radio or plug in your iSomething. Don't do it. Drive in silence. It's hard to do.

Silence contains a tremendous power and wisdom that we keep out of our lives intentionally. Isn't that dumb? The purpose of silence is to feel. The purpose of silence is to be instead of do. The purpose of silence is to listen.

The pursuit of wisdom is perhaps the greatest pursuit in the human experience, and wisdom comes from listening first. You can listen by reading books or asking hard questions of wise friends. Wisdom comes from silence too. Mother Theresa once said, "God cannot give to hands that are already full." God cannot give us experiences when we are too busy with our own schedules. Isn't it also possible that we can't hear wisdom if we've got the volume turned up too loud with our own conversations, podcasts, and music?

Seek out silence in your daily life. Turn off the radio in your car. Sit in silence while you drink your morning coffee. There is so much to be heard in silence.

ACTION TIP:
Put a note on the power button of your car stereo to remind you to keep it off for the next few days. Pay attention to the tension of silence. Listen.

Smirk

You should smile in the morning. I prefer to smirk. Smirking gets a bad rap.

We smile when what we thought was going to happen happens, because saw it coming. We smirk to ourselves because our foresight is like an inside joke. It's a hidden joy we don't show off with a full smile.

I smirk when I see something that no one else sees.

I smirk when I know an inside joke.

I smirk when I know I'm going to win.

I smile when good things are coming.

When you wake up early, you should smile because the day just got sucker punched. (Thanks to my friend Jon Acuff for the sucker punch idea.) You are smiling because you are ahead of the game, and you've jumpstarted your day with serious momentum.

Smile because you're in on the joke, and the joke's not on you — the joke is on your day. It never saw you coming. You sucker punched it.

One last reason to smile. You're proud of what you've achieved. You should be. I'm proud of you, too.

ACTION TIP:
Smile more.

DAY TWENTY-TWO

Partner Up

Invite your spouse to rise early tomorrow with you. (If you're not married, you can keep reading.)

Don't say:

I've been really disciplined, and you should wake up like me, you lazy bum.

You get plenty of sleep, so you can get up early just like me.

Do say:

I'd love to spend some time with you in the quiet of the morning.

I'd like to help you grow spiritually and personally, so can we get up early together tomorrow?

Experience the challenge together. You don't even need to talk to each other. In fact, it might not be a good idea to talk that early!

If you're not married, I encourage you to find a friend to meet for coffee very early tomorrow morning. It might sound crazy, but meeting with friends very early in the morning is a great way to start the day. I prefer to have very early coffee meetings because it starts my day well.

Let me know how it goes on Twitter or EarlyToRiseBook. com/Contact.

ACTION TIP:

Write an invitation for your spouse to join you tomorrow morning, and put it an envelope. Make it look formal because it's a big deal! If you're not married, call a friend and invite them to coffee. It's good to hear a friend's voice, so don't send a text or an email.

Write

One of my heroes is Andy Andrews. He has sold millions of books, but more importantly, he is a great human being. One would think this best-selling author loves to write, but on the podcast I host for him, he told me he actually hates to write. What he loves is to have written. Maybe you think you're a writer, and maybe you don't. Either way, I encourage you to spend some time writing in your early mornings. Write for yourself, for your kids so they have memories cataloged, or for an audience that one day may pay for your work.

I don't love to write, but I do love seeing the word count on a page and knowing God gave me thousands of words about a topic which will undoubtedly help others. I write because the lessons I learn would be wasted if I didn't share them. It's been said you learn your best lessons from your mistakes. That may be true, but I'd rather learn from other people's mistakes than from making them myself. Perhaps you can keep others from experiencing some pain by talking about your mistakes as well as your triumphs. People want to be understood and to feel a connection with an author. You could be that author. There is material or a story in you, but you have to do the work of writing it down.

If you think you may be a writer, I encourage you to pick up Jeff Goins' book, *You Are A Writer*. EarlytoRiseBook.com/YouAreAWriter. That book and a writing course he created called Tribe Writers are the reasons you're reading this book. It was just an idea until Jeff encouraged me and taught me how to publish it.

No one knows what their legacy will be, but I hope to be remembered for the wisdom I passed on to others. If that sounds egotistical, don't you want to make a difference too? Don't you want to help future generations avoid mistakes and live and love better than you have? George Santayana once said, "Those who cannot remember the past are condemned to repeat it."

If nothing else, write to leave a legacy for your family. That is no small thing. My children will remember the lessons of my past, because they will be able to read their dad's books and listen to his podcasts.

Let me know if you decide to write something. I would love to encourage you in your journey. You can reach me at EarlyToRiseBook.com/Contact.

ACTION TIP:
Write down twenty ideas for a book. Pick two, and set a goal to write 1,000 words a day for the next ten days. A 10,000 word count is about forty printed pages. You will be well on your way to writing a book, or you can take your forty pages and publish as a Kindle single.

Reacting

What would your life be like if you didn't initiate anything? What if you only reacted?

You would:

» Never set an alarm clock.

» Never speak without being spoken to.

» Never reach out to shake someone's hand first.

» Never ask your wife how she's feeling.

» Never tell your children they are special without them asking you first.

» Never volunteer to help someone.

» Never start a story on a blank piece of paper.

» Never seek a new job, church, or friendship.

A life of reacting is a life out of your control. Is that what you want?

When we check our email several times a day, we are living a reactive life. We are waiting for someone to call our name, and then we answer them. Sometimes we initiate messages, but when we check our inbox, we are ultimately asking if anyone wants to talk to us. We are seeking a feeling of importance. We are hoping we are needed. When messages come in, we feel needed, and we react by replying. When no messages come in, we feel unneeded and alone. The same is true of "likes" on your Facebook post, text messages, or cards in the mail on your birthday. When we wait for someone else to reach out to us, we are living a reactive life. Receiving is a beautiful thing, but it's only half of the communication equation.

Reacting is part of life, but if all we do is react, we will live very different lives than we would as creators and initiators. A creator initiates projects, ideas, art, conversations, friendships, gatherings, and movements. Creators make the world go round. Without creators, we would all be waiting for something to happen. Some of their plans fail, but we don't mind because they'll try something again soon. Initiate a conversation with a stranger by complimenting them. Initiate playing with your kids instead of them asking you. Initiate a difficult conversation that you've been putting off.

On a very practical level, don't check as often to see if you got an email or if someone "liked" your Facebook post. Take that energy, and initiate a phone call to a friend or say a prayer for your children, spouse, or a hurting situation in our world. Check those electronic messages every hour, or better yet, just a few times a day. I check Facebook once, perhaps twice a day, because I have a life to live offline.

The first step to creating more is to stop consuming what other people have already created. You can initiate and create, or you can react and consume. Which do you choose for today?

ACTION TIP:
Check your email once an hour today, and see if the world ends as a result.

DAY TWENTY-FIVE

Spread the Word

This experience has been a mostly private journey so far.

Today I want you to:

» Tell five people you're getting up early, and tell them specific ways your life has changed since you started this experience.

» Tell them where to get this book. Start at EarlyTo-RiseBook.com/Amazon.

Sharing your journey will create accountability for you to continue rising early. If you tell your friend at work you've been getting up at five o'clock, she might think you're nuts. She will probably also be impressed, so the topic is likely to come up again. You don't want to have to tell her you failed, so now you have some accountability.

You will inevitably change lives because a few of your friends will get the book and go through the experience. They will get up earlier to read, listen, pray, write, and be still. They'll become better boyfriends, spouses, friends, church members, and employees.

It is fun to take journeys with other people. In 2010, Seth Godin published a book entitled *Linchpin: Are You Indispensable?* Before I even finished reading it, I emailed him and asked his permission to create a podcast in which I discussed the book and interviewed linchpins. He graciously agreed as long as I called it The Unofficial Linchpin Podcast.

I don't know if he's listened to any of the dozens of episodes, but that wasn't the point. I read the book and wanted to share the experience with others. Since then, the show has been downloaded more than 250,000 times. When you share about your Early To Rise experience, you will find kindred spirits. We can never have too many kindred spirits.

Who are five people you will talk to today about the Early to Rise experience?

1.

2.

3.

4.

5.

ACTION TIP:
Did you complete your list? Tell those five people today about the experience.

Loneliness

Have you found other people taking this journey with you? Maybe you searched Twitter for mentions of #EarlyToRise and realized there were other people as crazy and dedicated as you are. It's also possible that no one joined you. The truth is that waking up early isn't going to sweep the nation like a hip fad. It's not hip. It's not easy. It's not appealing to most people.

Most people are apathetic. They don't believe they have a lot of control over their life.

Most people are inherently lazy, and I include myself in this group. I am lazy by nature, but through this experience, I've changed my life and become much more disciplined and productive.

Most people don't want to sacrifice anything. Again, we're programmed to do less, not more. When I got married, I didn't think I would need to change much. Man, was I wrong! I was selfish in so many ways, and my wife helped me see those parts of me so I could change them.

Most people don't want to sacrifice their habits or way of life. They may not like getting up at the last minute and arriving ten minutes late everywhere they go but they're not unhappy enough to actually change. They're content with creating little and reacting to everything around them. They could gain control to some degree, but they don't want to sacrifice anything to do so. They live lives of chaos and then call it normal because it is. Normal is also lame.

You are not those people. You've changed your life forever because you've changed your actions, which has resulted in a changed mindset. You will never be the same, whereas most people will mostly stay the same.

If you feel like you're on a lonely path, it's a sign you're different. You're unique. You're special. You're strong. You're dedicated. If you feel alone, it might be because you are. The top of the mountain is not crowded, because it's hard to get there. If you feel alone, it's because you're working every day to achieve something great. Wouldn't you rather feel alone while on the path to success than share the fellowship of the unmotivated?

If you feel alone, enjoy it. You're going the right direction.

ACTION TIP:
Buy yourself a special treat to eat during your time tomorrow morning. It will give you something to enjoy during your alone time, and it's a reward for your dedication thus far.

Think Again

Today's wisdom was written by my friend and Daniel Goldak. You can follow him on Twitter at Twitter.com/Dgoldak.

There's something in your life you don't like right now. It could be your job, your spouse, a friend, or your church. (We should love our spouses, but sometimes we don't like them. Sometimes they don't like us either. It's normal.)

This morning, try changing your mindset about whatever you don't like. Taking action is the best way to change how you feel about something, so make a list of the good things about whatever or whomever frustrates you right now.

> » I enjoy the customers I work with.
> » I like it when my wife gets up for our crying son in the night because I have to work early in morning.
> » I like that my boss gives me feedback instead of never telling me how I can improve.
> » I like the amount of energy my two-year-old daughter has.
> » I appreciate the friendships I have at my church.

If you think everything about your situation stinks, get back to the basics. Even if you hate your job, consider the fact that your paycheck has never bounced. (If your paycheck has bounced, start looking for a new job!) Focus on the small things your spouse does around the house.

Start looking for the positive instead of the negative — it's there if you look for it.

If it is people you dislike instead of a situation, do something positive for them. Go out of your way to help them. Give them a gift. Pray for their success. Choose to change your mindset by taking action in that direction.

ACTION TIP:
Buy a small gift for someone you've had conflict with in the past. A small gift card to a place they like to eat would be a simple and kind gesture.

Talking to No One or The One (God)?

You may have noticed in this book that I reference God and church occasionally. If you and I have had the pleasure of exchanging email, you may have noticed I end my emails with "Blessings." When I was fifteen years old, I discovered God wanted to walk with me throughout my life. Up to that point, He had been near when crisis came — which was rare — but otherwise kept His distance. I should say, I kept my distance from Him. After a July day in 1993, I began to walk with God.

My relationship with God is different from my other relationships, because I don't have God's cell number and He's not on Facebook. The only way I know how to communicate with Him is to pray, and that's what I'm inviting you to do. Have you ever called someone who didn't pick up the phone? You just left a message. Sometimes it feels good just to leave a message. God is totally okay with you leaving a message. You can thank Him for your beautiful family or ask Him why you've had so much pain in your life lately. He can take anything you throw at Him. He just wants you to talk to Him.

I've never heard God respond audibly to me, but I have seen Him answer prayers time and time again through provision and protection. He has even brought clarity to my thinking when I needed it.

Let me be clear: praying can be difficult. Praying can feel like talking to someone you can't see (and you're not even sure is there) on the other side of a wall. Worst of all, even if someone is there, they don't communicate in the same way you do.

So, let me make this really, really simple. God cares about you, so tell God what you're worried about. Ask Him for peace to get through it and the wisdom necessary to find solutions, then thank God for the good things in your life.

Perfect people are no fun, because they're hiding something. Don't play that game — be honest with God. You can pray for me too. I could always use the help.

ACTION TIP:
Start thinking of a way to treat yourself for your last day. Email me with your celebration plans at EarlyToRiseBook. com/Contact.

DAY TWENTY-NINE

My Birthday

On my sixth or seventh birthday, I had an *E.T.* cake. The movie, *E.T. the Extra-Terrestrial*, was very popular at the time, and I was a big fan. My parents bought me an *E.T.* cake and took a picture for me to remember the moment. Birthdays are a big deal when you're a kid.

Last week, I turned thirty-five. You know what I did for my birthday? I bought myself lunch. My wife has the ridiculously challenging task of caring for our three kids under five-years-old while I'm at work all day, so I didn't expect anything from her. I bought myself a nice lunch, and the next day, we had some really good cake at my mother-in-law's house.

As we get older, not every birthday will be amazing. In the same way, not every morning will yield great insights and profound moments of peace. This morning, I had about forty-five minutes to myself before my daughter woke up and came downstairs. Because of the distraction, I only wrote about one day's content of the thirty-day challenge. The rest of the day, I wrote twelve days worth of this book, so obviously her waking up slowed me down a lot. Life happens. Don't be too hard on yourself. Keep showing up every day, and great ideas will show up eventually too.

Invest in yourself every morning of this challenge so you can have an above average life. You can be above average in the areas of wisdom, patience, love, peace, kindness, faithfulness, and self-control. If you were above average in those areas of life, you would be a great person. You would reach your potential.

Don't be average. Average is lame.

ACTION TIP:

If you've done any writing during your morning times, share some of it with someone you trust. It will be difficult, but it's important that your words get shared with someone else.

The Last Day

Did it work?

» Did it work?

» Did you work?

» Did you change your life in the last thirty days?

» Did you and Fred become buddies?

» Did you learn to turn off the television more often?

» Did you learn to check your email less often?

» Did you create something your kids will appreciate when you're gone from this world?

» Did you start a project?

» Did your relationships improve?

» Do you tell your days who's in charge?

» Has your life changed?

I hope this experience has equipped, empowered, and encouraged you to take permission to change your life. If you paid for this book, you blessed me and my family through that exchange. Thank you. If you read this book and took action, you blessed the whole world. Yup, little old you changed the world just by listening to Fred early in the morning.

You've had quite the experience. See you in the morning.

ACTION TIP:
Repeat for the rest of your life.

THANKS

The best thing you can do to help me is change the world. You can change the world by getting up early and doing something significant.

The second best thing you can do to help me is tell a friend about this book or give him or her a copy. I wrote it at coffee shops and at my little office in Sioux Falls, South Dakota. I don't have a publisher; I have a computer and a good Internet connection. Every copy goes to help my wife and I raise our kids and, hopefully, buy a boat. (Just kidding about the boat. We live in South Dakota. Six months of the year, we need sidewalk salt and gasoline for our snowblower, not a boat.)

The last thing you can do is leave a review where you bought this book. Be honest, please. I just want people to know how or if this book changed your life.

Read, listen, and connect. You can find all my writing, speaking, and digital lessons at TakePermission.com. You can follow me at Twitter.com/AndyTraub. You can "like" me at Facebook.com/TakePermission. You can hear me talk about all sorts of topics by searching for my name on iTunes.

Thank you and bless you.

— Andy Traub, January 3, 2013,
Take Permission Media Network Headquarters
Sioux Falls, South Dakota

WHERE IT STARTED

The idea for a thirty-day Early To Rise Experience comes from a chapter in my friend Andy Andrews' book *Mastering the Seven Decisions*.

With his permission, I created thirty daily emails to help anyone learn how to rise early. Hundreds of people signed up for the challenge in the first few weeks, and the feedback was very powerful. Marriages improved, parenting became more joyful, and businesses grew. Those emails have been rewritten and compiled into the book you're holding in your hands.

I want to thank Andy Andrews for the idea for this experience, and I encourage you to listen to his podcast *In The Loop with Andy Andrews*. He's a great author and an even better friend.

CONNECT WITH THE AUTHOR

This is where you learn more about the author, but writing in third-person feels strange. It's my book, so here's how I do it:

- » I used to stare at the sun but never became blind. I guess my parents were wrong.
- » I'm horrible at a lot of things: details, delegating, growing facial hair, turning off my screens, listening more than speaking. I'm working on all of those things.
- » I have arguments with my wife.
- » I feel like a fraud half of the time and a genius the other half.
- » I read more words in Seth Godin's books than in the Bible. I'll let you judge me however you want.
- » I want to be a great father, and this book is part of that attempt.
- » I'm — at times — a dumb husband, but I'll always be married to the same woman and that's worth something.
- » I check my email WAY too much.
- » I buy things with an Apple logo without hesitation.
- » I'm a Christian but I'm embarrassed of most Christians.
- » I may struggle with some pride issues, but I'm too prideful to know for sure.
- » I don't think I want my kids to go to college.

- » I will die someday, but this book will still be spreading.
- » I believe you will change the world. God doesn't make mistakes, and He made you. Make something wonderful: your kids, your marriage, your work. Make them all with care.

Connect with Andy at:

Take Permission Media Network — TakePermission.com

Twitter — Twitter.com/AndyTraub

Twitter — Twitter.com/#EarlyToRise

Facebook — Facebook.com/TakePermission

Email — Andy@EarlyToRiseBook.com

THE EARLY TO RISE EXPERIENCE FOR MOMS

In order to help moms learn the habit of rising early, I teamed up with dozens of moms to write *The Early To Rise Experience For Moms* and *More Early to Rise Experience for Moms*.

» EarlyToRiseBook.com/Moms.
» EarlyToRiseBook.com/MoreMoms

CPSIA information can be obtained
at www.ICGtesting.com
Printed in the USA
FSOW02n0934031216
28130FS